Hitty's Goose

Written by Hawys Morgan

Illustrated by Ray Shuell

Collins

Hitty and Grandad were in the sleigh, racing across the ice. Hitty's fingers and thumbs felt numb with cold. Winter was coming.

The peace and quiet was broken by loud honking. It echoed around them. Hitty glanced up at the sky.

Thousands of geese were flying in a V-formation. Hitty exclaimed, "All the snow geese are travelling in the same direction!"

"It is their great migration south. The geese make this journey every winter," said Grandad.

It was a magnificent scene.

Suddenly, Hitty spotted a grey smudge on the ice.
They stopped and trudged over.

"It's a gosling – a baby goose!" whispered Grandad.
"Something is wrong with its wing."

Grandad knew all about wildlife. "Snow geese are fascinating. They fly to the same location in the Arctic Circle every year, then lay their eggs.

A day after the eggs hatch, the geese and goslings walk for days. They travel in a huge procession to find plants to eat," Grandad explained.

The gosling's parents must have left in the migration south.

"It's in danger here — a fox or even a whale might hunt it," said Hitty.

They took the decision to wrap the gosling in a knitted blanket and take him home.

Hitty nursed the gosling, feeding him crumbs and grass. Every week, she measured him and watched him grow plumper. She named him Barley because that was the food he liked best.

Soon, Barley's muscles became stronger. He bounced happily over the rocks and ice. He swam in the water, but he still wasn't able to fly.

Love and affection grew between Hitty and Barley.
He followed her everywhere. He even watched her play
ice hockey at school.

At the end of winter, Hitty and Grandad were exploring an old shipwreck. Hitty climbed the massive anchor. Barley tried to follow, but it was too high.

He stretched his wings and flew. Hitty hugged him.
"You can fly!" she smiled.

Then, thousands of geese flew overhead.
Barley honked excitedly. Hitty's happy emotions were
replaced with worry and sadness.

"Maybe Barley wants to find his family. Should we let him go? What's your advice, Grandad?" asked Hitty.

"He's a wild bird, but I know you treasure him. It's your decision, Hitty."

17

"Now he can fly, I'm sure it's wrong to keep him,"
said Hitty. "Barley is not my possession; he's not a toy.
He deserves freedom."

A smile stretched across Grandad's wrinkled face.
"I'm proud of you, Hitty."

18

"Remember me, Barley!" called Hitty. She let him go and he flew up into the sky.

Every year, Barley returned to visit Hitty, eventually bringing his own little goslings!

Hitty's diary

October

I found a fluffy, grey gosling!
His wing is hurt.

November

I named him Barley.
He can walk now.

December

Barley swam for the first time! He eats lots of grass. He has turned white.

January

Today was funny. Barley watched me play ice hockey.

February

I feel happy and sad. Barley flew for the first time and joined his family.

 After reading

Letters and Sounds: Phases 5–6

Word count: 499

Focus phonemes: /n/ kn /m/ mb /r/ wr /s/ c, ce, sc /c/ x /zh/ s /sh/ ti, si, ssi, s

Common exception words: of, to, the, into, are, said, were, their, today, because, great, water, parents

Curriculum links: Geography, Science, PSHE

National Curriculum learning objectives: Reading/word reading: apply phonic knowledge and skills as the route to decode words, read common exception words, noting unusual correspondences between spelling and sound and where these occur in the word; read other words of more than one syllable that contain taught GPCs; Reading/comprehension: develop pleasure in reading, motivation to read, vocabulary and understanding by being encouraged to link what they read or hear to their own experiences

Developing fluency

- Your child may enjoy hearing you read the book.
- Take turns to read a page of the main text, encouraging the use of different voices for each character.

Phonic practice

- Focus on the /s/ or /sh/ sounds in these words. Ask your child to read them and identify the letters that make the /s/ or /sh/ sounds:

  sure   fascinating   excitedly   direction   circle   procession

- Challenge your child to think of other words ending with "tion". You could prompt by saying, e.g. which word begins with, e.g. ac – action, instruc – instruction, fic – fiction, competi – competition.

Extending vocabulary

- Challenge your child to think of dictionary definitions for the following words: **migration** (e.g. *to go from one place to another*); **eventually** (e.g. *after a long time*); **fascinating** (*very interesting*)
- Take turns to point to another word and decide on a simple definition together.